BATTLE
GOD'S ARMOR

PUT ON THE FULL ARMOR OF GOD

Helmet of Salvation

Prayer

Breastplate of Righteousness

Belt of Truth

Shield of Faith

Sword of the Spirit (God's Word)

he readiness that comes from the ospel of peace

Majorie Daka

Scripture marked KJV are taken from the KING JAMES

VERSION (KJV): KING JAMES VERSION, public domain

Printed in the United States of America

ISBN:9781712298848

CONTENTS

INTRODUCTION

Many people have talked about prayer and there are numerous books written on the subject. It's true; we have amassed a great knowledge base with an arsenal of concepts and terminologies but are seemingly losing the battle for strategic spiritual warfare. This is simply because prayer is a practicum, and its' fruit is incumbent upon how much you engage in it. Although someone is familiar with what prayer is; they may not know how to effectively engage in art of prayer.

CHAPTER 1

What is spiritual warfare?

Spiritual warfare is an invisible war that is staged in the spiritual realm everyday - between humanity and spiritual forces.

To be effective in this war, there are weapons that God has given us in his word as stated in Ephesians 6:10-18.

These weapons include: The belt of truth, the breastplate of righteousness, the shoes of the gospel of peace, the shield of faith, the helmet of salvation, the sword of the spirit and all kinds of prayer. Since this is a spiritual warfare, our weapons are not carnal, but they are mighty through God with the ability to destroy demonic strongholds in our minds, in our cities and in our nations (1 Corinthian 10:4).

Therefore, carnality has no part in the victory that comes through using God's weapons. In Romans 8:7, the Bible states that carnal mind is enmity to God or to spiritual things. Therefore, it is impossible to fight this invisible enemy with our intellect, human wisdom and understanding. This war is fought in the spiritual realm and we are spiritual beings living in human bodies. On the other hand, this battle is not won by power or by might, but by the spirit of the Lord (Zechariah 4:6). The Holy Spirit is the greatest intercessor and instructor when it comes to waging spiritual warfare (John 14:26). With the help of the Holy Spirit, you can develop a customized plan of action for strategic prayer; as everyone has a designated life path with different challenges. Also, the Holy Spirit searches the deep things of God. (1 Corinthians 2:10).

CHAPTER 2

<u>Why do we fight?</u>

In Genesis 1:26-28, God created man and put him in charge of the earth, so he could rule after the heavenly pattern. God specifically said that man was to be fruitful, multiply, replenish, subdue, have dominion, live a healthy life and be productive. This means that God gave absolute power to man over the earth and his creation- works of his hands.

Psalm 8: 6 (amp)

You have made him have dominion over the works of your hands. You have put all things under his feet.

Prior to this, in Ezekiel 28:15-17, the Bible indicates that there already had been a battle between the kingdom of darkness and the kingdom of light when iniquity was found in Lucifer. So, man was created after spiritual battle had already begun. Therefore, we must understand that this war and battle belongs to the Lord (2 Chronicles 20:15). It must be fought according to God's rules of engagement. We must choose which side we will be fighting on; the kingdom of darkness or the kingdom of light. What is your side?

In Genesis; Chapters 1and 2, man was given the power and dominion to rule the earth. But through deception, Lucifer became the god of this world. Man relinquished his authority and as a result, became responsible for the condition of the earth and all the illegal demonic activities (Genesis 3).

Before man sinned, the earth had no thorns and thistles. Sin changed the molecular structure of the soil and produced thorns and thistles (Genesis 3:18).

The holiness or the righteousness of man affects the production of the land. In the book of Proverbs 14:34, the Bibles states that righteousness exalts a nation, when the people praise and worship God, the earth yields her fruit. For the land to go back to producing as God intended, we must get back to holiness and to worshipping the only true God. The book of Romans states that the earth is groaning waiting for redemption and the manifestation of the true sons of God (Romans 8:19-22).

Returning to the fear of God (Proverbs 9:10) and the worship of God (John 4:24) determines the production of the land, fruitfulness and harvest. Man has a mandate to fight for the place he lost in the earth so that God's will is done in the earth as it is in heaven (Matthew 6:10).

We are warriors and we must fight from God's side according to his rules of engagement, by putting on the whole Armor of God. The Amor is of God just as much as the battle is his. You and I were not there when this war all begun and so it is just wise to follow God prescribed way of winning this battle because him alone knows how to. The armor is also known as the armor of light (Romans 13:12). Therefore, just by putting it on, you literally switch on that divine light in your life that the devil cannot comprehend. In addition, it is the spiritual dress code for battle. (Ephesians 6:10-18).

It must be dressed as per prescribed by God words, failure to which victory is not guaranteed. God designed the armor for our benefit and it's very effective. Each piece of the armor is a dimension in which can stage war and win.

For example: The sword of the spirit is the word of God. When we declare it and obey it, victory follows because the word of God is active, quick and sharper than any two-edged sword.

It is amazing how Paul, the Apostle used the analogy of a Roman soldier to explain the pieces of the armor that can be used in staging spiritual battle. The Roman soldier was identified by his full armor.

This armor set him apart and distinguished him from civilians. The whole armor was designed with both the defensive and offensive mechanism for effective guard against the enemy's devices in battle confrontation.

Each piece of armor is significant and has a specific assignment it fulfills in the confrontation. Therefore, it's imperative to know what a specific armor represents, covers, and protects to use them effectively with expected results.

When the whole armor of God is properly applied, it will transform a believer into a weapon of power that can cause great damage to the kingdom of darkness (Romans 13:14).

The Armor of God is the dress code for spiritual warfare warriors, and every believer enlisted in God's Army. Prayer is the highest calling for every believer and there are no special people called to the ministry of prayer in the kingdom of God. Every believer is a soldier of the cross who's required to put on the whole Armor of God.

If we house God, we are called to be a house of prayer, or a house of spiritual battle (1 Corinthians 3:16, Isaiah 56:7). The dress code elevates the wearer to function in the dynamic power of God (Acts 4:30-31). It shows that we are standing in divine service.

As believers, we have all the necessary tools to have direct combat with the enemy and establish dominance in the earth because it is our territory (Ephesians 1: 21).

We are seated in the heavenly places far above principalities and power (Ephesians 2:6), which gives us the authority to enforce laws and pronounce legal judgment over a territory. We have the power to decree a thing and it is established right there and then (Job 22:28). Our jurisdiction power orders the earth and heaven to drive the enemy out of our territory.

Any illegal demonic activities going on in the earth realm simply indicates the level of dominion enforced. We are responsible for the illegal demonic activities because this is our territory, as previously stated, this is our jurisdiction.

We are the spiritual law enforcement agents who should be about arresting all the demons and reinforcing order and peace in our land. The level of order and peace in our communities, cities, and nations is a clear indication of where we are in our spiritual warfare. It's time to arise.

Now looking at the full armor of God, as stated in Ephesians 6:10, we will discover that it covers specific body

parts that have specific spiritual
significances.

The pieces of the armor of God in a
successful spiritual warfare has the
assignment to help you stand up against
all the schemes, strategies, tactics, and
deceits of the enemy, and enforce
heavenly kingdom rule in the earth.

CHAPTER 3

<u>The belt of Truth</u>

Stand therefore having your loins girded about with truth (Ephesians 6:14).

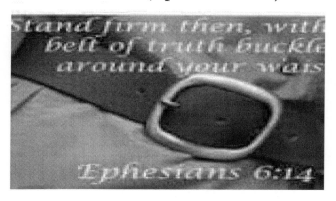

This piece of armor is called the belt of truth that should be around your waist protecting your loins. To "gird "means to prepare for a dangerous situation, in this case, the battle. In ancient times, men would gird their loins when preparing for battle.

Loins are related to reproductive organs (Genesis 35:11). They are connected to personal integrity and moral courage. Engaging in sexual immorality and all manner of sexual perversion opens the door to a landslide defeat (1 Thessalonians 4:3-5).

It is a quickest way of demonic transfer. How interesting is that the first piece of the armor is that which relates to our morality and sexual purity. The truth about our intimacy with God is very crucial in this spiritual battle because we cannot fight on the side of the king we have no intimate relationship with. In Isaiah 11: 5, the Bible states that righteousness will be the belt around his loins and faithfulness the belt around his waist (our Lord Jesus Christ).

According to the word of God, the truth must dwell in you to stage a victorious spiritual warfare (Colossians 3:16). The belt of truth also points us to the Lord Jesus Christ. In the gospels, Jesus stated that he is the truth and as such he must dwell in us to set us free and position us on the platform of victory (John 8:32). In martial arts, when one is belted, is a sign of rank or achievement. This rank is achieved by winning different levels of fights. But our God gives us the belt of truth even before we engage in many fights because our Lord Jesus Christ won the war, and as such, we are not fighting for victory, but we are fighting from a place of victory. This is why we called more than conquerors (Romans 8:37). We are already ranked as victors. The belt of the truth is a defensive armor against deception and lies of the enemy. As previously stated in Genesis chapter 3, man fell and lost his dominion and authority because the truth was distorted by Satan through the serpent.

Therefore, for us to go back to that place of power authority, and dominion Jesus is the way and the truth that will leads and keep us at that place of dominion. Our lives are hidden in Christ Jesus (Colossians 3:3).

As a believer, you cannot have other gods and expect to win the battle. Choosing other gods instead of the only God of truth, which is Jesus Christ, provokes war in the gates and paves the way for defeat.

Whenever the children of Israel chose other gods, defeat was at their doorsteps (Judges 5:8). Therefore, sexual purity, righteousness and faithfulness determine your victory against the devil; your intimacy with God must be guarded and protected with the truth.

What Truth? The truth that we are made in the image of God (Genesis 1:26, 27) and that we are destined to rule and reign with Christ. This is the truth that gives us the liberty to soar and stage spiritual warfare without fear.

To be free or be at liberty simply means not being physically or spiritually restricted. Therefore, this piece of armor guards your loins, sexuality, identity and image. Remember, Lucifer convinced himself that he was a god trapped in the body of an angel (Ezekiel 28:2). He thought more highly of himself than he needed to and that led to his miserable defeat.

Demonic attacks can sabotage our power and cripple us in the battle for authority through prayer - convincing us that we are trapped and without Christ-like authority and dominion. The enemies goal is to strip us our identity so we're powerless against sexual immorality and perversion (Matthew 19:4-6). Engaging in spiritual warfare without knowing the truth of: who we are in God, who God is, and who our enemy is; is tantamount to spiritual suicide.

When looking at a Roman soldier, the belt around his waist had pouches that carried different types of weapons, these represent the word of God with different scriptures that we can draw out and use during specific confrontation with the enemy. For example: Jesus was tempted about the food and he pulled out "Man shall not live by bread alone (Matthew 4:4), and when he was tempted about worship he pulled a different word which said, "Worship the Lord your God, and serve him only" (Matthew 4:10).

Jesus Christ is the manifested truth and word of God. He is all we need to win.

In him, we live and move and have our being (Acts 17:28).

CHAPTER 4

<u>Breastplate of Righteousness</u>

And having on the breastplate of righteousness (Ephesians 4:14).

The Breastplate of righteousness covers the chest cavity protecting the lungs and the heart. The chest cavity signifies the Ark of the Covenant, the residence of God's breath and the manifestation of God's glory. Righteousness allows us to stand before God, before man and before the enemy with confidence. It is not something we earned but was given to us by Jesus Christ who is our righteousness (Romans 3:22).

The breastplate of righteousness also protects the heart from incidental harm and unplanned hazards that arise because of not being fully equipped. In the book of Proverbs 4:2, the Bible clearly states that you should guard your heart with all diligence for out of it are issues of life.

As Christians, every decision made must align with the word of God to avoid these hazards. Living right and walking in holiness protects the breath of God (lungs) in us and controls the outflow of our mouth (heart). From the abundance of the heart, the mouth speaks, (Matthew 12:34).

In addition, righteousness keeps the presence of God and the breath of him activated. When we put on the Breastplate of righteousness, you secure the glory of God for your battle. We cannot win the spiritual battle without the presence of God. This battle belongs to the Lord (1 Samuel 17:47). During the days of Eli, the children of Israel lost the battle against the Philistines when they carried the Ark of the Covenant to the battlefield because of sexual sin (1 Samuel 4:3-10).

The sins of Hophni and Phinehas caused the glory of God to depart from Israel because they were sleeping with women who assembled at the entrance of the tent of meeting (1 Samuel 4:22

and 1 Samuel 2:22).

This shows that it is very important to have the glory of God with you when going in to battle as an individual or as a nation. Proverbs 14:34 states, righteousness exalts a nation, but sin is a reproach to any people.

To *exalt* means to elevate, promote or advance. This lets us know that righteousness can elevate or promote and saves, but also kills if not properly worn. The unrighteous act of two priests brought about reproach to the nation, not elevation. This goes first, to husbands, who are priests of their homes. Your unfaithfulness to your spouse creates an Ichabod in your home and opens your home to demonic invasions. Secondly, all believers are priests (Revelation 1:6), and sexual sins (fornication, adultery and all kind of sexual perversions) create an Ichabod in our lives and paves a way for quick transfer of demons into our lives.

Therefore, the Breastplate of righteousness points to:

- Walking in holiness, which means to be in right standing with God.
- Secures your victory.
- Positions us to walk in authority.
- Positions us for different dimensions and levels warfare.

CHAPTER 5

<u>Shoes of the gospel of peace</u>

And your feet shod with the preparation of the gospel of peace (Ephesians 6:15).

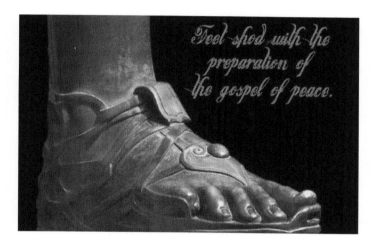

The gospel of peace should be the assignment of your feet. Preaching the gospel is an offensive weapon that directly provokes the enemy to battle. In Romans 10:15 and Isaiah 12:7, the Bible states that beautiful are the feet of those

who bring good news. Feet are apostolic
foundation on which the house of God
is built (Ephesians 2:20). Bringing good
news is simply preaching the gospel and
win souls for the Lord because souls are
at the center of God's kingdom. It is his
desire that none should perish but
receive eternal life (John 3:16). In John
17:2-3, Jesus prayed to his Father and
encouraged that he would give eternal
life to as much as he could because
power upon all flesh has been given to
him.

However, the preaching of good news-
the Gospel - attracts persecution
because it is the power of God (Romans
1:16) and it is offensive against the
kingdom of darkness. Like he washed
his disciples' feet, the Lord Jesus Christ
must wash your feet and qualify you for
the mission. The Bible says that you are
clean by the words I speak (John 15:3).

Jesus is the Word that cleans our foundations so that we are ready to face the challenges out there as we preach the gospel and prepares us to tread upon territories before taking the journey. This is a soul winning journey. To take this journey and yield an expected result, we must be a disciple of Jesus Christ (John 13:5-3, Joshua 1:3).

Remember, the enemy does not want the gospel of truth to be preached because it depopulates his kingdom. During combat, shoes are worn for protection and defense. They provide stability, especially when crossing spiritual rough landscapes of life. We cannot wear the shoes of the gospel of peace if are not part of him and he is not part of us because he is peace (Colossians 3:15). His goal is to create one new man from all the seven continents of the world, thus the

breaking of barriers (Ephesians 2:15).
Today, there is no Jew or gentile,
circumcision or uncircumcision, male or
female and bond or slave (Galatians
3:28, 1 Corinthians 7:19). Our
foundation must be rooted in God
before we can arise and walk the walk
(1Corithians 3:11).

The gospel of peace gives us the ability
to be peace negotiators in the earth as
we advance the gospel through Jesus
Christ, who is the prince of peace
(Isaiah 9:6).

This piece of armor represents your
assignment:

- To be on the move, to go out and
  preach the gospel
- Walk in the light
- To carry and bring good news
- Prepares us for combat

- Gives you stability and flexibility for effectiveness in battle
- Good footing that brings victory

CHAPTER 6

<u>Shield of Faith</u>

Above all taking the shield of faith wherewith ye shall be able to quench all the fiery darts of the wicked (Ephesians 6:16)

Faith is having complete trust and confidence in something. In Hebrews 11:6, the Bible states that it is impossible to please God without faith. This simply means that we cannot even engage in this battle if you don't believe in God. Faith in God pleases him.

Apostle Paul encourages us to gear up (To equip oneself) for battle with the shield of faith in your left hand. The left side depicts weakness and the right depicts the strength. In other words, when you feel weak in this battle, use your faith and trust God but when you feel strong, use the word and fight. The sword of the spirit which is the word of God is held in the right hand. This shield is an active protective device and a deception blocker designed to put away any fiery darts of the enemy that causes doubt, discouragement, and unbelief. Shields vary in sizes.

The least size of the faith you can have is that of a mustard seed. This smallest size of faith can move mountains.(Matthew 17:20).

For example: David killed Goliath, a giant that everyone feared, because he trusted in God and he declared it as he approached the giant (1 Samuel 17:40-51). He wore his faith well because of previous successes he had with the help of God when he killed a lion and a bear (1 Samuel 17:34-36).

David's relationship with God, the word of God and private challenges sharpened, trained and enhanced his faith which brought about heroism on the battlefield for the entire nation.

Difficult situations in life may require different levels of faith but every level or size of faith must be rooted in the word of God, or else it wouldn't be able to function and produce results. We grow our faith by reading the word of God and having a relationship with God.

Every believer has been given a measure of faith and every day it must be watered by the word of God to grow (Romans 12:3). Faith is a powerful extinguisher God has given a believer to intercept attacks of the enemy. It comes by hearing and hearing by the word of God (Romans 10:17). Hence faith simply means picturing it done right now.

Hebrews 11:1 shows that faith is the evidence of things not seen, bringing the spiritual 'invisible' in to the natural 'visible'. It is having complete reliance on what you have not seen physically but seen spiritually. As kingdom ambassadors of Christ, we are privileged to exercise our faith in battle and provide God with the platform to show up (2 Corinthians 5:20).

The Bible admonishes us to whether our Lord Jesus Christ will find faith on earth when he returns (Luke 18:8).

This simply means while we are waiting for his return, we must remain in his faith and put him on during battle, because he is our shield of faith. Paul also said that he had fought a good fight of faith (2 Timothy 4:7-8). We must contend for our faith in God because faith pleases God (Jude 3:1).

We are to grow from faith to faith and glory to glory. Put on the faith today and fight. This piece of armor of God gives the believer the ability to:

- Ward off the arrows of deception, doubt or fear.

CHAPTER 7

<u>The helmet of Salvation</u>

And take the helmet of salvation (Ephesians 6:17).

The helmet of salvation is the fifth piece in the armor of God. The number five signifies grace, favor and life.

In the Hebrew alphabet, it symbolizes inspiration, illumination and revelation knowledge.

The helmet protects our head (authority) and mind (battlefield) so that the enemy doesn't undermine our authority and build strongholds in our mind. Strongholds hinder progress.

Therefore, having the helmet of salvation secures our battlefield, and positions us for victory and protects your mind from evil thoughts. The mind is the starting point of all wars. Get the mind in the game.

Paul encourages to be transformed by the renewal of our minds (Roman 12:1-2). The mind must be renewed (resumed, rewired)daily for our daily battles. The mind works like a computer and it needs to be cleaned up daily, so it uploads the word of God in readiness for the next encounter. The mind functioned perfectly before man sinned but now it requires daily renewal to be fit for battle (Genesis 1:27). Through his blood and his word, Jesus reinstated our mind to its original state bringing salvation as God, his Father intended (Philippians 2:5). Salvation is deliverance from sin (2 Timothy1:9). New thought patterns are required to win the battle.

In Philippians 4:8, the Bible lists the things we must think about. What is on your mind? Isaiah 26:3, states that he will give you perfect peace when your mind is stayed on thee.

We must guard our minds from the worldly influence to be effective in battle. A negative mind undermines its own strength and impairs the capacity to win the battle. The word of God equips us to create spiritual landmines that can destroy the enemy with explosive power of destruction. Because the word of God renews our minds, the enemy will always attack God's word and snatch it from you to create unbelief, doubt and confusion. He used the same strategy on Eve and succeeded. When he used it on our lord Jesus Christ, he failed miserably. Therefore, it is imperative that we study the word of God daily as our spiritual food. In Isaiah 59:17, the Bible states that God puts on the helmet of salvation, even if he is God; who is all powerful. He is a man of war, so he leads by example (Exodus 15:3). If God wears his armor, we have no excuses for not wearing it especially that we are full of shortcomings. We are saved by grace, granted to us through our Lord Jesus, thus connecting us to eternal life (Ephesians 2:8). Jesus Christ is the only door that secures our enlistment in the army of the Lord.

CHAPTER 8

<u>Sword of the Spirit</u>

... the sword of the Spirit, which is the word of God (Ephesians 6:17).

A sword is a bladed weapon intended for slashing or thrusting, cutting and piercing. The word of God is known as the sword of the spirit. The spiritual warfare we are enlisted in is a warfare of

swords. In sword wars, speed, skill and efficiency are required for desired results. In Hebrews 4:12, the Bible states that the word of God is sharper than any two –edged sword, active and quick. It judges the thoughts (mind) and attitudes of the heart (heart) so much that it penetrates in every way.
It is both offensive and defensive.

It is defensive when used to counterattack the plan of the enemy and when used to protect us from the schemes. It is offensive when drawn out to have a direct combat with the enemy. Since we are on our journey to heaven, we are constantly fighting demons to make our elect sure. Therefore, we must saturate our lives with the word of God.

The purpose of the sword of the spirit (word) is to make us withstand against all forces of darkness opposing us.

For us to win, we need the power of the Holy Spirit (Acts 1:8). The word of the Lord is tried, and he is a buckler to all those that trust in him (Psalm 18:30).

CHAPTER 9

<u>Prayer</u>

Praying always with all prayer and supplication in the Spirit and watching thereunto with all perseverance and supplication for all saints. (Ephesians 6:18)

Prayer is an ancient activity of talking to God, which is an offensive weapon just like the sword of the spirit. It activates everything and brings revelation to what we are fighting against. Prayer engages the enemy. Prayerlessness legalizes demonic activities.

Upon putting on the whole armor of God, prayer takes us to the battlefield. It becomes the springboard that helps us to bounce higher at the level we want.

Prayer breaks limitations and ushers us into different dimensions of breakthroughs. As we remain vigilant, it breaks strongholds of the enemy and paves way for God to intervene.

Because Prayer is a spiritual activity, one needs strength from God. (Isaiah 40:31). It is not enough to just put on the armor of God; you must engage the enemy through prayer, to establish dominion in whatever territory God has given us (Genesis 1:28).

Dominion means having control over a place, which means that you determine what should happen in that territory. We have authority to allow and disallow. As stated earlier, as humanity we are responsible for what is happening in the earth because the earth is our territory and we have allowed the enemy to terrorize us and hold us hostage in our territory.

When we engage in battle, we must be under the power and authority that we possess through our Lord Jesus (Luke 10:19). What power do you possess?

The enemy's assignment is to disengage us from the root of prayer and dislocate us from the power source, so we can become ineffective (Daniel 6:11-12). To be effectual in prayer, we must maintain

an intimate relationship with our Lord
Jesus Christ.

Our covenant relationship with God
gives him the legal right to operate on
behalf of the earth (Psalm 34:17). It is
God's kingdom that should be
established in the earth. As previously
stated, we must gain ground and
repossess territories on his behalf and
establish his rule. Prayer brings heaven
on earth (Daniel 10:12).
The Apostle Paul always encourages us
to pray in all occasions in the spirit and
be alert (Ephesians 6:18). Every time we
go into prayer, we are entering the
courts of God. Psalms 100:4 states that
we must enter his gates with
thanksgiving and his courts with praise.

This is the protocol for approaching
God, the righteous judge as we enter in

to present our case. During the spiritual hearing through prayer, we must understand and know how to interpret the heavenly constitution to fight to win our case and counterattack the accusations of the enemy.

The heavenly constitution is the Bible, the word of God (1 Peter 1:25). It must dwell in us richly so that we are able to argue our case before God and defeat the accuser of the brethren-Satan (Revelation 12:10).

Reading and studying the word of God is a key strategy to equip us with enough endurance to present before God. Besides that, the word of God is the sword that we use to thrash against the enemy.

THE AUTHOR

Prophetess Majorie Daka was born in Zambia in the southern part of Africa. She came to know the Lord Jesus Christ via a visitation in 2006.

prophetess Majorie loves the Lord with all her heart, mind and soul and her passion is to see the lives of individuals transformed and set free from bondage by the power of God.

In the year 2010 Prophetess Majorie
founded Kingdom Way Ministries
(KWM), a nonprofit organization with
the vision to train the people of God in
spiritual warfare strategies and tactics
for personal and corporate spiritual
advancement.

Through Kingdom Way Ministries
(KWM), Prophetess Majorie empowers
the people of God to become effective
and productive citizens of the Kingdom
of God. She believes that this can be
accomplished when God's people
understand and know spiritual strategies
that gives the ability to penetrate
through the visible and invisible forces
that are assigned to hinder their
advancement in repossessing the
territories in the spiritual land of
Canaan.

Prophetess Majorie is an author who
has authored several books. She

continues to conduct her always sold out periodic Prayer and Strategic Warfare boot camps and Training seminars with her best seller book - BATTLE CODE- GODS ARMOUR (which can be bought on Amazon.com)

She is a firebrand deliverance minister and a much sought after conference speaker, an educator and entrepreneur. Three (3) words that encapsulate her ministry are Strategic, Empowering & Dimentionalist.

Prophetess Majorie speaks at different church conferences, Seminars and on weekly webinars and weekly radio Podcast.

Printed in Great Britain
by Amazon